The Sailboat and the Sea:

ENCOUNTERS WITH GOD THROUGH THE JOURNEY OF LIFE

STUDY GUIDE

Endorsements

I read a lot—not because I have to, but because I love to. And I absolutely love this book. Many people tend to write to show what they know and how much you don't know. But from page one I knew this was going to be a truly unique experience.

The Sailboat and the Sea is packed cover to cover with wisdom, but not the "I'm smarter than you" kind—more of a childlike wisdom. Anyone can understand what's being taught. Literally even a child could read this and "get it."

And that's the best kind of writing. I highly recommend this creative take on the relationship between you and your Creator.

—Robert Cook, Pastor, Author, Speaker and Disciple of
my Lord and Savior

Brilliantly written. Powerful. Relevant. Engaging. *The Sailboat and the Sea* skillfully represents two sides of God's immense capacity to shepherd us within his paternal and maternal characteristics. He meets us as a father: a protector, a disciplinarian. Then as a mother pouring out unconditional love, a gentle nurturer. When we can consciously draw upon the fullness of God as both father and mother, it is then that we become keenly aware of our completeness in him. In this delightful book, Peter Lundell captures the relentless human struggle during tumultuous storms, and illustrates the mighty yet loving heart of God that provides all of our needs. I saw myself throughout this endearing work.

—Carol L. Brooks, Author, *Uncharted Territory*

In trying to explain *The Sailboat and the Sea* to myself, I settled on *allegory*, although it can also be a book of tender devotional reads. It fits into the same category as Hannah Hurnard's story about Much Afraid in *Hinds' Feet on High Places*. Or Christian in John Bunyan's 400-year-old classic, *Pilgrim's Progress*.

The book is a dialog between LittleBoat talking to BigSea about the problems of life. The warm tones and obvious compassion shine through in such a way that readers readily realize *they are the little boat*.

—**Cecil Murphey**, author or co-author of more than a hundred books, several of which have appeared on the New York Times bestseller list. His titles include *90 Minutes in Heaven*, co-written with Don Piper and *Gifted Hands: The Ben Carson Story*.

This wonderfully creative and unique devotional book will deepen your relationship with the Lord. Each short chapter provides much Truth to ponder. Like LittleBoat you'll find yourself engaging in conversations with the Lord that will change your life. Highly recommended!

—**Marlene Bagnull**, Author, Speaker & Director of Write His Answer Ministries

Reading *The Sailboat and the Sea* has confirmed for me what I've always suspected: Peter Lundell is a Christian mystic. There is simply no other word that is apt to explain his uncanny connection between humanness and spirituality. With his masterful use of language, Peter forms a wonderful bridge helping us to move with effortlessly between those two worlds.

—**Michael Gantt**, Speaker, Missionary, Author, *Sharpening the Iron of the Church*

A practical self-examination, using an easy to understand and comprehend conversational format. This book challenges us to ask and review the tough questions and what might be our priorities as we move into the unknown future.

—**Chuck Fountain**, Louisiana District Superintendent, Church of the Nazarene

The Sailboat and the Sea:

ENCOUNTERS WITH GOD THROUGH THE JOURNEY OF LIFE

STUDY GUIDE

Peter Lundell

A sailboat encounters the sea for a
heart-and-mind-swirling journey with God.

PUBLISHING THE POSITIVE

ELK LAKE PUBLISHING INC.
Plymouth, Massachusetts

Cover and Interior Design: Derinda Babcock

Editor(s): Susan K. Stewart, Deb Haggerty

Author Represented by Credo Communications

PUBLISHED BY: Elk Lake Publishing, Inc., 35 Dogwood Dr., Plymouth, MA 02360, 2019

Library Cataloging Data

Names: Lundell, Peter (Peter Lundell)

The Sailboat and the Sea: Encounters with God through the Journey of Life Study Guide / Peter Lundell

70 p. 23cm × 15cm (9in × 6 in.)

Description: A sailboat encounters the sea for a heart-and-mind-swirling journey with God.

Identifiers: ISBN-13: 978-1-950051-09-0 (trade) | 978-1-950051-10-6 (POD) | 978-1-950051-11-3 (e-book.)

Key Words: sailing, inspirational, life, discovery, spiritual knowledge, self-discovery, devotional

Dedication

To Drs. Dan and MaryAnn Nusbaum,
who invited me to sail with them
across the middle of the Pacific Ocean
on their sailing vessel StarReach.
On that sailing trip
the ideas for this book were born.
Thank you, thank you, thank you.

The Sailboat and the Sea
STUDY GUIDE

How to Get the Most out of This Study Guide

Who is the Sailboat but a personification of you and me? Who is the Sea but a personification of God our Creator, Redeemer, and Lover of our souls?

This guide can be used individually or with a group, in which you'd share and interact on personal thoughts and experiences.

In this study guide let God speak to you directly from passages of Scripture about the same issues LittleBoat goes through. Refer to each chapter of the original book open as you go through to get the full combination of life context and Scriptural response.

Seeing yourself as LittleBoat, express what you would say to BigSea. Writing it down will give clearer, stronger expression to your thoughts and feelings.

Then imagine what God as BigSea might say back to you personally. Before or after you write that down, read the selected passage from the Bible about the topic. That may influence what you imagine God as BigSea might say.

Then go to the prayer starter and finish it in your own words, whether few or many, as kind of a prayer journal.

May you be blessed on your journey through life.

And don't forget to be a blessing to others!

Peter Lundell

The Sailboat and the Sea

1. Who Are You?

My Own Journey

What I would say to BigSea about who he is:

_____

_____

_____

What BigSea might say back to me:

_____

_____

_____

God Is Beyond Our Categories
Exodus 3:13–15

> Moses said to God, "Suppose I go to the Israelites and say to them, 'The God of your fathers has sent me to you,' and they ask me, 'What is his name?' Then what shall I tell them?"
>
> God said to Moses, "I AM WHO I AM. This is what you are to say to the Israelites: 'I AM has sent me to you.'"
>
> God also said to Moses, "Say to the Israelites, 'The LORD, the God of your fathers—the God of Abraham, the God of Isaac and the God of Jacob—has sent me to you.'
>
> > "This is my name forever,
> >   the name you shall call me
> >   from generation to generation."

Moses is fearfully responding to God's call to lead the Israelites out of Egypt. He asks God's particular name because in that world a god's name always indicated its nature or specialty. The one great true God is beyond all categories. He is the origin of all existence. So he tells Moses simply to call him "I AM." This is in Hebrew *Yahweh* (or YHWH). Moses feels small, like LittleBoat or like you and me, before this infinite God. Yet we find that this God communicates with us and cares for us.

Prayer Starter

Lord, you are above and beyond me, greater than any hardship I face or

anything I imagine. I welcome you into my life today.

_____

_____

_____

_____

_____

_____

_____

_____

_____

_____

_____

_____

2. Who Am I?

My Own Journey

What I would say to BigSea about who I am:

_____

_____

_____

What BigSea might say back to me:

_____

_____

_____

We Matter to God Because We Are His
John 1:12–13

> Yet to all who did receive him, to those who believed in
> his name, he gave the right to become children of God—
> children born not of natural descent, nor of human deci-
> sion or a husband's will, but born of God.

Compared to the world around us and its billions of people, each of us
is microscopic. We can do what we like to feel important, but to God
we're still a speck. Yet impressiveness doesn't matter. What matters is
relationship. When we enter into a covenantal relationship of faith, and are
"born again," God our Father loves us—and cares for us and puts up with
us—because we are his. And nothing can ever take that away.

Prayer Starter

My Father in heaven, thank you for loving little me. Thank you that I'm important to you because I'm yours.

_____

_____

_____

_____

_____

_____

_____

_____

_____

_____

_____

_____

_____

_____

_____

_____

_____

_____

3. Look What I Have

My Own Journey

What I would say to BigSea about my possessions:

_____

_____

_____

What BigSea might say back to me:

_____

_____

_____

Life Does Not Consist in the Abundance of Our Possessions
Luke 12:15–21

> Then he said to them, "Watch out! Be on your guard against all kinds of greed; a man's life does not consist in an abundance of possessions."
>
> And he told them this parable: "The ground of a certain rich man yielded an abundant harvest. He thought to himself, 'What shall I do? I have no place to store my crops.'
>
> "Then he said, 'This is what I'll do. I will tear down my barns and build bigger ones, and there I will store my surplus grain. And I'll say to myself, "You have plenty of grain laid up for many years. Take life easy; eat, drink and be merry."'
>
> "But God said to him, 'You fool! This very night your life will be demanded from you. Then who will get what you have prepared for yourself?'
>
> "This is how it will be with whoever stores up things for themselves but is not rich toward God."

Like this rich guy, we too often try to establish our self worth through amassing material possessions or accomplishments. God is not impressed. He knows they will distract us from truly important things. They'll even deceive us into thinking we don't need God. We can do everything economically that the world teaches or admires, yet if we are not "rich toward God," that is, putting our time, treasure, and talent into Kingdom-of-God kinds of things, he considers us fools—because he sees everything from the perspective of eternity.

Prayer Starter

God Almighty, may I be always awake and oriented to you and things eternal. Free me and keep me from trying to impress myself or anyone else with the abundance of my possessions or accomplishments.

_____

_____

_____

_____

_____

_____

_____

_____

_____

_____

_____

4. Life Stinks

My Own Journey

What I would say to BigSea about things I don't like:

_____

_____

_____

What BigSea might say back to me:

_____

_____

_____

It's Not What Happens That Matters, It's How We Respond
Acts 4:23–31

> On their release, Peter and John went back to their own people
> and reported all that the chief priests and the elders had said to
> them. When they heard this, they raised their voices together
> in prayer to God. "Sovereign Lord," they said, "you made the
> heaven and the earth and the sea, and everything in them. You
> spoke by the Holy Spirit through the mouth of your servant,
> our father David:
>
> > "'Why do the nations rage
> >   and the peoples plot in vain?
> > The kings of the earth rise up
> >   and the rulers band together
> > against the Lord
> >   and against his Anointed One ...'
>
> Now, Lord, consider their threats and enable your servants to
> speak your word with great boldness. Stretch out your hand to
> heal and perform signs and wonders through the name of your
> holy servant Jesus."

The Sailboat and the Sea

> After they prayed, the place where they were meeting was shaken.
> And they were all filled with the Holy Spirit and spoke the word
> of God boldly.

The disciples Peter and John had been arrested and threatened. But their response is not fear, complaint, retreat, or self-pity. They and the church rise up in bold defiance of the ungodly opposition. God's response of filling them with the Spirit and shaking the place demonstrates his pleasure at this positive attitude and faith. Likewise, when we've been beaten down, or face difficulties, but respond with faith and expectation, we can expect God to empower us as well.

Prayer Starter

Lord, regardless of whatever has happened to me, or whatever I face, I choose to respond by faith. I choose to act and believe with a positive mind and know you are with me.

_____

_____

_____

_____

_____

_____

_____

_____

_____

_____

_____

5. I Was Abused

My Own Journey

What I would say to BigSea about how I've been hurt in the past:

_____

_____

_____

What BigSea might say back to me:

_____

_____

_____

God feels our pain with us and receives it from us.
Psalm 34:15–19

> The eyes of the LORD are on the righteous
> and his ears are attentive to their cry;
> but the face of the LORD is against those who do evil,
> to blot out their name from the earth.
> The righteous cry out, and the LORD hears them;
> he delivers them from all their troubles.
> The LORD is close to the brokenhearted
> and saves those who are crushed in spirit.
> The righteous person may have many troubles,
> but the LORD delivers him from them all;

We've all been hurt emotionally. Some of us have been violently abused. It's hard to get past the pain and anger, both toward the perpetrator and toward God. But if we can grasp that the horror of a free life with pain is better than the horror of life as a controlled machine, perhaps we can know God is with us through all things. And as we know God's constant, caring presence, even when it hurts, we can believe and then receive his healing and deliverance from the pain.

Prayer Starter

Lord, during my hard times take me beyond asking why, and lead me into deep connection with you. I seek you and trust you as the healer of my heart. And I offer myself to be your agent of healing to others.

_____

_____

_____

_____

_____

_____

_____

_____

_____

_____

_____

_____

6. I Feel Rejected

My Own Journey

What I would say to BigSea about feeling rejected:

_____

_____

_____

What BigSea might say back to me:

_____

_____

_____

God always receives us; he calls us to receive others as well.
Psalm 68:5–6

> A father to the fatherless, a defender of widows,
>   is God in his holy dwelling.
> God sets the lonely in families,
>   he leads out the prisoners with singing;
>   but the rebellious live in a sun-scorched land.

We've all faced and felt varying degrees of rejection. It may be easy to think that God rejects us too. But God doesn't accept or reject by the same criteria as the world we live in. We are his in a covenantal relationship. His acceptance is absolute and unwavering. He is our Father, and within communities of believers we find family. So we only hurt ourselves if we in turn reject others or comfort ourselves with toxic self-pity. Better to forgive and receive our Father's embrace.

The Sailboat and the Sea

Prayer Starter

My Father, thank you for always receiving and embracing me. I say yes to that and to the spiritual family you have for me. I choose to renounce self-pity and to live in the freedom that comes in relationship with you.

_____

_____

_____

_____

_____

_____

_____

_____

_____

_____

_____

_____

_____

7. I'm Afraid

My Own Journey

What I would say to BigSea about my fears:

_____

_____

_____

What BigSea might say back to me:

_____

_____

_____

Not being afraid has everything to do with who's with us.
Mark 4:35–41

> That day when evening came, he said to his disciples, "Let us go over to the other side." Leaving the crowd behind, they took him along, just as he was, in the boat. There were also other boats with him. A furious squall came up, and the waves broke over the boat, so that it was nearly swamped. Jesus was in the stern, sleeping on a cushion. The disciples woke him and said to him, "Teacher, don't you care if we drown?"
>
> He got up, rebuked the wind and said to the waves, "Quiet! Be still!" Then the wind died down and it was completely calm.
>
> He said to his disciples, "Why are you so afraid? Do you still have no faith?"
>
> They were terrified and asked each other, "Who is this? Even the wind and the waves obey him!"

Sometimes fear can get the better of us, and when it does, it blinds us to God's presence and promises. Throughout Scripture, God tells us through prophets, angels, and Jesus himself to not fear. This exhortation has nothing to do with our circumstances getting better or being not so bad. It has to do with only one thing: whom we're with—or who's with us. Just as Jesus is in the boat with the disciples, he is in our life with us.

Prayer Starter

Lord, regardless of what I face or what causes me fear, I choose by faith, and will remind myself, to acknowledge and remember that you are in my boat with me. So I will not be afraid.

_____

_____

_____

_____

_____

_____

_____

_____

_____

_____

_____

_____

_____

_____

8. Been There and Done That

My Own Journey

What I would say to BigSea about humdrum, everyday life:

_____

_____

_____

What BigSea might say back to me:

_____

_____

_____

Let the wonder of God awaken within you.
Psalm 19:1–4

> The heavens declare the glory of God;
>   the skies proclaim the work of his hands.
> Day after day they pour forth speech;
>   night after night they reveal knowledge.
> They have no speech, they use no words;
>   no sound is heard from them.
> Yet their voice goes out into all the earth,
>   their words to the ends of the world.

In our busy and media-saturated world, our brains can get so oriented toward the constant barrage of information and entertainment that we live shallowly between distraction and amusement. We can lose interest, and even the physiological ability to find wonder and awe in the natural world as God created it. Yet at every level of the natural world, God's fingerprints are to be found. Blessed are those who awaken to God's pervasive presence and live meaningfully in it and among other people.

The Sailboat and the Sea

Prayer Starter

Lord, open my eyes. Open my ears. Open all my senses to you and your presence in this natural world. Take me beyond myself to live meaningfully with you and with others.

_____

_____

_____

_____

_____

_____

_____

_____

_____

_____

_____

_____

_____

_____

_____

_____

9. I Messed up. Is There Hope?

My Own Journey

What I would say to BigSea about how I've messed up my life:

_____

_____

_____

What BigSea might say back to me:

_____

_____

_____

Unlike what we deserve, God is merciful and forgives.
Luke 15:11–31

> Jesus continued: "There was a man who had two sons. The younger one said to his father, 'Father, give me my share of the estate.' So he divided his property between them.
>
> "Not long after that, the younger son got together all he had, set off for a distant country and there squandered his wealth in wild living ...
>
> "When he came to his senses, he said, 'How many of my father's hired servants have food to spare, and here I am starving to death! ...' So he got up and went to his father.
>
> "But while he was still a long way off, his father saw him and was filled with compassion for him; he ran to his son, threw his arms around him and kissed him.
>
> "The son said to him, 'Father, I have sinned against heaven and against you. I am no longer worthy to be called your son.'
>
> "But the father said to his servants, 'Quick! Bring the best robe and put it on him. Put a ring on his finger and sandals on his feet. Bring the fattened calf and kill it. Let's have a feast and

celebrate. For this son of mine was dead and is alive again; he was lost and is found.' So they began to celebrate."

Every human being who ever lived has messed up and fallen short of any worthiness before God. We've done it both willfully and unknowingly. Our sin separates us from God, and our disconnected relationship means we don't have the life of the Holy Spirit living in us—until we repent and receive Christ as Savior and Lord of our lives. And when we do, our Father in heaven is delighted, and great rejoicing resounds heaven.

Prayer Starter

Father, my loving heavenly Father, you love me when I don't deserve it, and you love me before I ever love you back. I receive your sacrifice for me, your forgiveness, and the new life you offer in a covenantal relationship with you .

_____

_____

_____

_____

_____

_____

_____

_____

_____

_____

_____

10. Can I Trust You?

My Own Journey

What I would say to BigSea about my ability to trust him:

_____

_____

_____

What BigSea might say back to me:

_____

_____

_____

Hardship and danger are God's classrooms of trust.
Isaiah 43:1–2

> But now, this is what the LORD says ...
>
> "Do not fear, for I have redeemed you;
>   I have summoned you by name; you are mine.
> When you pass through the waters,
>   I will be with you;
> and when you pass through the rivers,
>   they will not sweep over you.
> When you walk through the fire,
>   you will not be burned;
>   the flames will not set you ablaze."

We may hate when God allows—or seems to intentionally take us through—hardship. He lets us worry and fear, and he lets us suffer. In the process our pride and stubbornness is hopefully broken. And through that we learn to trust him more, even when it may seem he's not there. When (not if) we pass through flood or fire, he is with us. The more we think and act by faith, the more we can expect to see his hand at work.

Prayer Starter

Lord, whatever challenge I face, and through whatever I cannot see before me, I choose to trust in you. Give me the grace for that trust and to keep trusting.

_____

_____

_____

_____

_____

_____

_____

_____

_____

_____

_____

_____

_____

11. What Is the Truth?

My Own Journey

What I would say to BigSea about ultimate truth:

_____

_____

_____

What BigSea might say back to me:

_____

_____

_____

There really is an ultimate truth, and it's found in relationship.
John 14:5–6

> Thomas said to him, "Lord, we don't know where you are going, so how can we know the way?"
>
> Jesus answered, "I am the way and the truth and the life. No one comes to the Father except through me."

People have always looked, and will always continue to look, for philosophical or religious truths to guide them. Some believe all truths are relative, and they may be offended that Scripture claims to hold the ultimate truth, particularly as manifest in Jesus Christ, the incarnation of truth. Every person must choose. Unlike every other truth claim on earth that is basically a proposition or ideology, Jesus himself is the way, the truth, and the life. He alone is the valid person who made the valid sacrifice to connect us to God the Father.

The Sailboat and the Sea

Prayer Starter

Lord, lead me into profoundly knowing you as the way, the truth, and the life. Grant me the grace to experience what this means and how to live it out.

_____

_____

_____

_____

_____

_____

_____

_____

_____

_____

_____

_____

_____

_____

_____

12. What Is Love?

What I would say to BigSea about loving and being loved:

_____

_____

_____

What BigSea might say back to me:

_____

_____

_____

Love can hurt, and God's love for us hurts the most.
1 John 4:7–9

> Dear friends, let us love one another, for love comes from God.
> Everyone who loves has been born of God and knows God.
> Whoever does not love does not know God, because God is
> love. This is how God showed his love among us: He sent his
> one and only Son into the world that we might live through
> him.

The English word for *love* finds three expressions in the Bible's original Greek: physical (*eros*), emotional (*philos*), and the giving of oneself for the best interests of others (*agape*). We may be all-too-familiar with the emotional ups and down of being romantically in love, but God calls us beyond ourselves into his way of love—the giving of oneself. As we do, we empty ourselves in giving, and we grow in the character of God more than we could in any other way.

The Sailboat and the Sea

Prayer Starter

Lord, lover of my soul, teach me how to love as you love. Through all the sacrifice and all the joy, show me how to become love to you and to others .

_____

_____

_____

_____

_____

_____

_____

_____

_____

_____

_____

_____

_____

13. I Wonder

What I would say to BigSea about things I wonder about:

_____

_____

_____

What BigSea might say back to me:

_____

_____

_____

Forget normal. Free yourself to be in awe.
Psalm 89:5–8

> The heavens praise your wonders, LORD,
>   your faithfulness too, in the assembly of the holy ones.
> For who in the skies above can compare with the LORD?
>   Who is like the LORD among the heavenly beings?
> In the council of the holy ones God is greatly feared;
>   he is more awesome than all who surround him.
> Who is like you, LORD God Almighty?
>   You, LORD, are mighty, and your faithfulness surrounds you.

Solid biblical faith and orthodox doctrine are critically important for the spiritual well-being of every believer. But spiritual vitality requires more than facts, more than correctness. Opening ourselves to the infinite wonders of God, who exists in dimensions incalculably beyond us, awakens us to life and faith and wisdom and awe that point us, and sometimes take us, beyond the normality of this world.

Prayer Starter

Lord of the Universe, awaken a God-inspired wonder in me. Take me beyond dry correctness of facts or doctrine and into living it, breathing it, experiencing it. Lead me beyond words toward your inexpressible greatness

.

_____

_____

_____

_____

_____

_____

_____

_____

_____

_____

_____

_____

_____

_____

_____

_____

_____

14. I Want to Reach the Moon

My Own Journey

What I would say to BigSea about my ambitions:

_____

_____

_____

What BigSea might say back to me:

_____

_____

_____

Striving can be its own punishment, unless it's done God's way.
Hebrews 12:7–8, 11

> Endure hardship as discipline; God is treating you as his children. For what children are not disciplined by their father? If you are not disciplined—and everyone undergoes discipline—then you are not legitimate, not true sons and daughters at all ... No discipline seems pleasant at the time, but painful. Later on, however, it produces a harvest of righteousness and peace for those who have been trained by it.

The world we live in tends to always push us toward not just achievement, which is good, but dominating or being better than others, which produces great products and performances but leaves the people doing it in bondage to the constant push. That's exhausting. Better, and more enduring, to be the best we can be. That involves the personal growth that comes from enduring hardship. And lasting greatness in God's kingdom comes by giving, not by getting.

The Sailboat and the Sea

Prayer Starter

Lord, teach me to be the best *me* you created me to be—regardless of anyone else. When I face hardship, I will take it as your training. Fill me and meet my needs as I give myself and whatever else I can give to you and to others.

_____

_____

_____

_____

_____

_____

_____

_____

_____

_____

_____

_____

_____

15. Where Am I Going?

My Own Journey

What I would say to BigSea about my direction in life:

_____

_____

_____

What BigSea might say back to me:

_____

_____

_____

Getting lost is easy. Being with God, we're already found.
Psalm 73:23–26

> Yet I am always with you;
>   you hold me by my right hand.
> You guide me with your counsel,
>   and afterward you will take me into glory.
> Whom have I in heaven but you?
>   And earth has nothing I desire besides you.
> My flesh and my heart may fail,
>   but God is the strength of my heart
>   and my portion forever.

Sometimes we think we know what we're doing or where we're going in life. Then our circumstances change, we change, or hardships rise up. We can also get distracted and only afterward see how far off track we've gone. Some may forget about God altogether. There are endless ways to get lost. As we live by faith and not by circumstances, we will follow God increasingly well—and do it on the path he's given us. And not seeing the future is okay because we know whom we are with.

The Sailboat and the Sea

Prayer Starter

Lord, I can easily get distracted from my life's course as I live it each day. I can even get lost. I commit to receive your grace and to live and follow by faith.

_____

_____

_____

_____

_____

_____

_____

_____

_____

_____

_____

_____

_____

_____

16. I Wish

My Own Journey

What I would say to BigSea about things I wish for:

_____

_____

_____

What BigSea might say back to me:

_____

_____

_____

Daydream all you like, but being and giving of yourself is your best path.
1 Corinthians 12:14–22

Even so the body is not made up of one part but of many.

Now if the foot should say, "Because I am not a hand, I do not belong to the body," it would not for that reason stop being part of the body. And if the ear should say, "Because I am not an eye, I do not belong to the body," it would not for that reason stop being part of the body. If the whole body were an eye, where would the sense of hearing be? If the whole body were an ear, where would the sense of smell be? But in fact God has placed the parts in the body, every one of them, just as he wanted them to be. If they were all one part, where would the body be? As it is, there are many parts, but one body.

The eye cannot say to the hand, "I don't need you!" And the head cannot say to the feet, "I don't need you!" On the contrary, those parts of the body that seem to be weaker are indispensable.

The Sailboat and the Sea

How often we imagine being someone else, owning something else, achieving and being recognized beyond ourselves—or just longing for a past we romanticize. A life worth living happens right here, right now, with who we are—not who we're not. God has created each of us uniquely and with a worthwhile part in his kingdom. And as we live our part with selfless giving, we enter into true freedom and effectiveness.

Prayer Starter

Lord, spare me from the tendency of wishful comparison that so often leads me to covet or despair. I commit to live out the life you've given me. And in all I am and all I have, I will aim toward generous abundance.

_____

_____

_____

_____

_____

_____

_____

_____

_____

_____

_____

_____

17. I'm a Failure

My Own Journey

What I would say to BigSea about my failures:

_____

_____

_____

What BigSea might say back to me:

_____

_____

_____

We may feel like a failure, but God sees a fortune.
Romans 12:1–2

> Therefore, I urge you, brothers and sisters, in view of God's
> mercy, to offer your bodies as a living sacrifice, holy and
> pleasing to God—this is your true and proper worship. Do not
> conform to the pattern of this world, but be transformed by
> the renewing of your mind. Then you will be able to test and
> approve what God's will is—his good, pleasing and perfect will.

We often feel like a failure even when we really aren't. By nature, we fear
and hate failure. Yet we need to realize that success isn't necessarily the
wonderful thing we may assume it to be. Failure can mature and grow us
more than success can. So a wise person will embrace it and learn from it.
As we rework our definition of success, we can grow to the level where we
die to the dream of being a success and live to the dream of being a blessing.

The Sailboat and the Sea

Prayer Starter

Lord, I let go of all my failures and give them to you. But I also commit to learn and grow from them. Lead me to die to the dream of being a success and live to the dream of being a blessing.

_____

_____

_____

_____

_____

_____

_____

_____

_____

_____

_____

_____

_____

_____

_____

18. I Hurt

My Own Journey

What I would say to BigSea about emotional pain:

_____

_____

_____

What BigSea might say back to me:

_____

_____

_____

God feels our pain with us and calls us to let it go into him.
2 Corinthians 1:3–7

> Praise be to the God and Father of our Lord Jesus Christ, the
> Father of compassion and the God of all comfort, who com-
> forts us in all our troubles, so that we can comfort those in any
> trouble with the comfort we ourselves receive from God. For
> just as we share abundantly in the sufferings of Christ, so also
> our comfort abounds through Christ. If we are distressed, it is
> for your comfort and salvation; if we are comforted, it is for
> your comfort, which produces in you patient endurance of the
> same sufferings we suffer. And our hope for you is firm, because
> we know that just as you share in our sufferings, so also you
> share in our comfort.

We all feel some kind of hurt, whether physical or emotional. And when
we do, let's always remember that God feels our pain with us, even if he
doesn't take it away. Letting go of emotional pain can be scary, but God
calls us to give it to him—and we have to—if we are to receive his healing.
After we do so, we in turn may become God's agents of healing for others.

The Sailboat and the Sea

Prayer Starter

Lord, I put both my physical pain and my emotional pain into your hands. I release it all to receive your healing. And as I do, may I in turn become to others an agent of your healing.

—————————————————————————

—————————————————————————

—————————————————————————

—————————————————————————

—————————————————————————

—————————————————————————

—————————————————————————

—————————————————————————

—————————————————————————

—————————————————————————

—————————————————————————

—————————————————————————

—————————————————————————

—————————————————————————

—————————————————————————

—————————————————————————

—————————————————————————

19. I'm Stressed Out

My Own Journey

What I would say to BigSea about things that cause stress:

_____

_____

_____

What BigSea might say back to me:

_____

_____

_____

Stress is one way God talks to us.
Philippians 4:6–7

> Do not be anxious about anything, but in every situation, by
> prayer and petition, with thanksgiving, present your requests to
> God. And the peace of God, which transcends all understand-
> ing, will guard your hearts and your minds in Christ Jesus.

Sometimes we take René Descartes' dictum, "I think; therefore, I am," and change it to say, "I'm busy; therefore I am." In our contemporary world we all too easily attach our self-worth to keeping ourselves busy. God sees through all that and calls us to focus on what's important. As with all our other burdens, we also release our stress to him. When we take time for rest and peace in him, we will enter renewed vitality.

Prayer Starter

Lord, keep me from the deception of thinking busyness equals meaningfulness. When I feel stressed, I commit to take it as your nudging me to reduce and to rest. And my deepest rest is in you.

_____

_____

_____

_____

_____

_____

_____

_____

_____

_____

_____

_____

_____

_____

_____

_____

_____

_____

_____

20. I'm Angry

My Own Journey

What I would say to BigSea about feelings of anger:

_____

_____

_____

What BigSea might say back to me:

_____

_____

_____

Be careful with your anger, and remember who's the judge.
Romans 12:17–21

> Do not repay anyone evil for evil. Be careful to do what is right in the eyes of everyone. If it is possible, as far as it depends on you, live at peace with everyone. Do not take revenge, my dear friends, but leave room for God's wrath, for it is written: "It is mine to avenge; I will repay," says the Lord. On the contrary:
>
> > "If your enemy is hungry, feed him;
> >   if he is thirsty, give him something to drink.
> > In doing this, you will heap burning coals on his head."
> > Do not be overcome by evil, but overcome evil with good.

We all get angry at times. But is it self-centered anger, or is it righteous anger that leads us to do good on another's behalf? Usually it's the first. And how long do we stay angry? We may justify our feelings, but we only hurt ourselves. As God is the ultimate judge, we dare not take his place. And because he's the ultimate judge, we are free to trust judgment to him, which enables us to let go of anger—and that sets us free.

The Sailboat and the Sea

Prayer Starter

Lord, the next time I get angry, don't let me off the hook. I must release it into your hands, for you are the ultimate judge, and you free me from the bondage of unforgiveness. Lead me from there to overcome evil with good.

_____

_____

_____

_____

_____

_____

_____

_____

_____

_____

_____

_____

_____

21. I'm Lost in the Storm

My Own Journey

What I would say to BigSea about feeling lost in life:

_____

_____

_____

What BigSea might say back to me:

_____

_____

_____

God takes us through storms, not out of them.
Isaiah 45:2–4

> I will go before you
>   and will level the mountains;
> I will break down gates of bronze
>   and cut through bars of iron.
> I will give you hidden treasures,
>   riches stored in secret places,
> so that you may know that I am the LORD,
>   the God of Israel, who summons you by name.
> For the sake of Jacob my servant,
>   of Israel my chosen,
> I summon you by name
>   and bestow on you a title of honor,
>   though you do not acknowledge me.

Storms of life can really freak us out. And when they do, we have a hard time thinking through our theology or our walk with God. That's why we should prepare ourselves ahead of time to trust, hold on, believe, move forward, and not quit when things get tough. When the time comes, God may let us go through all kinds of trauma to where we might be angry at him or doubt him. Yet his hand is still with us.

Prayer Starter

Lord, as I face storms and obstacles in life, teach me to trust beyond my fears. In the midst of trouble, I choose to see your hand that holds and strengthens me.

_____

_____

_____

_____

_____

_____

_____

_____

_____

_____

_____

_____

_____

_____

_____

_____

22. I'm Worn Out

My Own Journey

What I would say to BigSea about being exhausted:

_____

_____

_____

What BigSea might say back to me:

_____

_____

_____

Deep, rejuvenating rest requires a decided yes to God's invitation.
Matthew 11:28–30

> "Come to me, all you who are weary and burdened, and I will
> give you rest. Take my yoke upon you and learn from me, for I
> am gentle and humble in heart, and you will find rest for your
> souls. For my yoke is easy and my burden is light."

The idea that rest takes determination may seem odd, but life can be filled with so many demands, opportunities, and distractions that to truly enter deep rest, both physically and mentally, we must do it by conscious decision. If we assume it will just happen, it probably won't—or our body (even our mind) will break down because it needs rest. Jesus, even in the activity of serving him, offers us the deepest and most rejuvenating rest.

The Sailboat and the Sea

Prayer Starter

Lord, in both my tiredness of body and weariness of soul, I choose to come to you and take your yoke upon me rather my own or any of the world. I receive your deep rest that rejuvenates my soul.

_____

_____

_____

_____

_____

_____

_____

_____

_____

_____

_____

_____

_____

_____

_____

_____

_____

_____

23. This Is Not What I Expected

My Own Journey

What I would say to BigSea about feeling disillusioned:

_____

_____

_____

What BigSea might say back to me:

_____

_____

_____

Whatever happens, do it with God.
Habakkuk 2:13–14

> Has not the LORD Almighty determined
>> that the people's labor is only fuel for the fire,
>> that the nations exhaust themselves for nothing?
> For the earth will be filled with the knowledge
> of the glory of the LORD,
>> as the waters cover the sea.

By mid-or-late life, it's easy to feel disappointed if we haven't achieved some expectation of wealth or achievement. And even if we do, we may feel a nagging emptiness. Yet in all we go through in life, as we do it not apart from God, or for God, but rather with God, we'll gain a greater sense of meaning and of purpose. Also when we do things with God, they'll likely be of lasting value.

The Sailboat and the Sea

Prayer Starter

Lord, whatever I expected in life, or still expect, I determine to put into your hands. I will not do things apart from you, or for you. I will do things with you.

_____

_____

_____

_____

_____

_____

_____

_____

_____

_____

_____

_____

_____

_____

_____

24. I'm Lonely

My Own Journey

What I would say to BigSea about feeling lonely:

_____

_____

_____

What BigSea might say back to me:

_____

_____

_____

Loneliness is never lonely when we meet God in it.
Deuteronomy 31:8

> "The LORD himself goes before you and will be with you; he
> will never leave you nor forsake you. Do not be afraid; do not
> be discouraged."

We may sometimes feel that God is absent because he is quiet. But remember
that every believer in Christ is in a covenantal relationship with God, and
he will never leave or abandon us. Loneliness is among the best situations
in which to connect deeply with God, and as we do, the loneliness turns
into intimate communion. That blessing in turn flows from us to create
more friendship with others.

The Sailboat and the Sea

Prayer Starter

Lord, when I feel lonely, that's the best time to meet you. In my times of loneliness, I commit to spending them with you.

_____

_____

_____

_____

_____

_____

_____

_____

_____

_____

_____

_____

_____

_____

_____

_____

_____

_____

_____

_____

_____

25. Where Is My Value?

My Own Journey

What I would say to BigSea about the value of my life:

_____

_____

_____

What BigSea might say back to me:

_____

_____

_____

Our greatest value is in what we give.
2 Corinthians 9:10–11

> Now he who supplies seed to the sower and bread for food will
> also supply and increase your store of seed and will enlarge
> the harvest of your righteousness. You will be made rich in
> every way so that you can be generous on every occasion, and
> through us your generosity will result in thanksgiving to God.

This false notion is as subtle as it is universal: To gain a sense of personal worth, we need to be like someone else or have what they have. But regardless of who we are, God values us as his children. In living that out, our greatest value is not found in accumulating but in giving. The more we give away, both of what we have and of who we are, and the more we empty ourselves for others as Jesus did, the greater is our personal value and sense of value.

The Sailboat and the Sea

Prayer Starter

Lord, keep me from false notions that I have to be like someone else to be worth anything. Lead me into the fullness of experiencing how giving of myself becomes my greatest value.

_____

_____

_____

_____

_____

_____

_____

_____

_____

_____

_____

_____

_____

_____

26. Where Does It End?

My Own Journey

What I would say to BigSea about how my life will end:

_____

_____

_____

What BigSea might say back to me:

_____

_____

_____

Our end is no end at all, but a new beginning.
1 Corinthians 15:50–57

> I declare to you, brothers, that flesh and blood cannot inherit the kingdom of God, nor does the perishable inherit the imperishable ... For the perishable must clothe itself with the imperishable, and the mortal with immortality. When the perishable has been clothed with the imperishable, and the mortal with immortality, then the saying that is written will come true: "Death has been swallowed up in victory."
>
> "Where, O death, is your victory?
>
> Where, O death, is your sting?"
>
> The sting of death is sin, and the power of sin is the law. But thanks be to God! He gives us the victory through our Lord Jesus Christ.

Our life's end opens a new beginning, and not knowing our end is a merciful thing. Imagine how the knowledge would debilitate us. Yet we are wise to prepare ourselves by living each day here and now with eternity in our hearts and minds. We have so much to look forward to, more and better than we can imagine, as our mortality will be transformed into immortality in the very presence of God.

Prayer Starter

Lord, may I always be mindful that this life will end, and that it will continue in eternity. And may that anticipation fill me with continual joy.

_____

_____

_____

_____

_____

_____

_____

_____

_____

_____

_____

_____

_____

_____

27. The Enveloping Sea

My Own Journey

What I would say to BigSea about the reality of dying:

_____

_____

_____

What BigSea might say back to me:

_____

_____

_____

A believer's death and entry into heaven is precious to God.
Psalm 116:15–16

> Precious in the sight of the LORD
>   is the death of his faithful servants.
> Truly I am your servant, LORD;
>   I serve you, just as my mother did;
>   you have freed me from my chains.

None of us will get out of this world alive. From earth's point of view, death may be a grievous end, but from God's point of view, the earthly death of every believer is a precious heavenly event, a welcome into life beyond our imagining. And we will be free, more than we could ever imagine.

The Sailboat and the Sea

Prayer Starter

Lord, fill me so much with a sense of eternity that when my time is done, I do not fear. I have only joy as I anticipate eternity with you in all its fullness and freedom.

_____

_____

_____

_____

_____

_____

_____

_____

_____

_____

_____

_____

_____

_____

_____

_____

_____

_____

_____

_____

28. Your Chapter

My Own Journey

What I would say to BigSea about anything else:

_____

_____

_____

What BigSea might say back to me:

_____

_____

_____

How will you live your life?
Galatians 2:20

> I have been crucified with Christ and I no longer live, but
> Christ lives in me. The life I live in the body, I live by faith in
> the Son of God, who loved me and gave himself for me.

We all choose how we live our lives, but our choices determine our paths.
If we submit to the death of our carnal selves, particularly the passions and
desires, we may live with the fullness of God's Spirit in us. Many believers
don't fully live this way, but those who do enter into a life of identification
with Christ that has no limits except those that we may impose. This is life
in the Spirit.

The Sailboat and the Sea

Prayer Starter

Lord, crucify, put to death in me, everything carnal and not of you. Fill me with your Spirit. Live in me, transform me, and lead me step by step in this continually new life.

_____

_____

_____

_____

_____

_____

_____

_____

_____

_____

_____

_____

_____

_____

_____

_____

_____

_____

_____

_____

_____

_____

About the Author

DR. PETER LUNDELL found the inspiration for Sailboat and the Sea while on the crew of a 45-foot sailboat across the Pacific. His hope is those who read this book will have a greater appreciation for the wonder of the world, of life, and its Creator. Peter teaches and mentors people who want to go deeper into the spiritual side of their journeys.

Also by Peter Lundell ...

Prayer Power

30 Days to a Stronger Connection with God

www.ingramcontent.com/pod-product-compliance
Lightning Source LLC
Chambersburg PA
CBHW060147050426

42448CB00010B/2348